S0-DGG-549

The Main Thing

...

Katie Pates

Copyright © 2017 Katie Pates

Unless otherwise indicated, all Scripture quotations are taken from the Holy Bible, King James Version (KJV).

Scripture quotations marked "NIV" are taken from the Holy Bible, New International Version®, NIV®. Copyright © 1973, 1978, 1984, 2011 by Biblica, Inc.™ Used by permission of Zondervan. All rights reserved worldwide. www.zondervan.com. The "NIV" and "New International Version" are trademarks registered in the United States Patent and Trademark Office by Biblica, Inc.™

ISBN: 1978047169
ISBN 13: 9781978047167

"For Christ also hath once suffered for sins, the just for the unjust, that he might bring us to God, being put to death in the flesh, but quickened by the Spirit."

1 PETER 3:18

Table of Contents

Introduction

• • •

Much of the Church today is like the ancient church at Ephesus, mighty in her works and faithful and diligent in her service but deficient. The deficiency? "Nevertheless I have somewhat against thee, because thou hast left thy first love" (Revelation 2:4).

Look at the Church today. Look at the failed marriages, adultery, and the divorce rate among Christians. Look at the stress and the addictions. Look at the unwise decisions. Look at the growing debt and financial impropriety. Look at the scourge of abortion. Look at the prevalence of heresy and apostasy. Look at Christian leaders, once mighty in the faith but now deposed in horrific scandals. Look at the state of our nation, once Christian but now in serious peril from threats both within and without. Above all, look at the fact that our children and grandchildren are not walking with God and are either leaving the church outright in droves or remaining in it but living in open or silent rebellion. All these things are true across denominational lines. We are all guilty. Our situation is truly desperate.

Every modern Christian should tremble at the exhortation that Jesus Christ gives to such a church. "Remember therefore from whence thou art fallen, and repent, and do the first works; or else I will come unto thee quickly, and will remove thy candlestick out of his place, except thou repent" (Revelation 2:5). The Church today is truly in danger of having its candlestick removed. We mourn that this possibility seems so imminent. But we are not there yet. There is hope.

Jesus Christ tells us if we remember where we have come from, repent, and return to "the first works," we will be secure. This book has been written to address a particular need my family has perceived within the Church at large today. We are convinced that the Church needs to return to the main thing, which is God, and learn to abide with Him personally, as a family, and corporately within the body of believers. We are convinced that Christians must recognize the Gospel — the death, burial, and resurrection of Jesus — does not merely secure our eternal destiny but has brought us to God and has made it possible for us to enjoy a relationship with God *now*. We are convinced that this relationship encompasses our entire life and reforms our soul from within so we, in turn, can give and reach out to others. We are convinced that the Church must be Word-saturated, worship-empowered, and Spirit-filled so individuals and families can deliberately dedicate themselves to abiding with God. Then, things change. People change. Families change. Churches change. Neighborhoods change. Towns change. Cities change. States change. Nations change. Worlds change. We have seen it happen.

For these reasons, my mother wrote this book for her twelve children, her future grandchildren, and her great-grandchildren to a thousand generations. My father fully supports and agrees with everything in this book. If you are holding this book as a descendant, please know that my parents have been praying for you and believing the promises of God for you: "Know therefore that the LORD thy God, he is God, the faithful God, which keepeth covenant and mercy with them that love him, and keep his commandments to a thousand generations" (Deuteronomy 7:9). Both my parents want their children and grandchildren to understand that the foundation for Christianity is anchored upon the Gospel of Jesus Christ alone. Christ died to pay for our sins to make a way for us to have a relationship with the Triune God because He is perfectly holy and would otherwise have been unapproachable by sinners. God is the main thing. Keeping God and His glorious Gospel in laser focus is radically transforming our family. We have to say no to many good things to keep the main thing the main thing. My mother has taught us how to arrange our entire lives around the God we love and reach out to the people God continually brings into our lives to love. This book explains what my mother and father want their children to know about the Gospel and how the finished work of Christ on the cross brings us to God.

My parents want us to recognize that true biblical Christianity is not rule keeping. Rather, a true Christian is a person who has a saving relationship with God and pursues God for God. It is not to obtain the blessings of God, a mere ticket to heaven when we die, or for any other motive. God is what a true Christian should want more than anything else. True Christians have an insatiable desire to know God more and more because pure joy and perfect peace is found in this lifelong relationship. My mother wrote this book to help us understand how our relationship with God thrives through quality time spent with Him individually, as a family, and with His church.

As our family has invested time in each of these spheres with our God, we have grown closer to Him and to each other. My parents have a beautiful marriage. They love, honor, respect, and cherish one another deeply. My father and mother are full of joy when they see happy children who love their parents, love each other, and most importantly love their God. Our home is bursting at the seams with joy, laughter, generosity, learning, organization, beauty, hospitalities, Sabbath celebrating, Christmas partying, gourmet cooking, delicious desserts, real butter, crisp bacon, good wine, cute cupcakes, hot coffee, gummy bears, prayer walks, fun runs, thankfulness journals, cowhide Bibles, daily devotionals, shelves of great books, Bible recordings, catechism reciting, Psalms sung in harmony, yo-yoing, piano playing, banjo picking, guitar strumming, drum banging, powerful praying, family worship gatherings, girl talks, boy talks, Gospel love, and grace. We all love it here! Indeed, God has been gracious and kind to our family, but His greatest gift to us is the Gospel. The Gospel is the very power of God Himself, and that is changing us and changing everything!

Our family does not profess to have all the answers or recommend a specific lifestyle, a set of activities, or a list of "do's" and "don'ts" as the ultimate solution. We are just like you – sinners in need of a Savior. There is lots of sin in our home, but because God has extended grace, mercy, and forgiveness to all of us, we extend grace, mercy, and forgiveness to each other. People who see our family at church, during hospitalities, or in public may sometimes think that no sin exists here, but that is not true. Forgiveness is a nonstop activity in our home. We forgive huge sins and small misdemeanors. All fourteen of us get into sin on a daily basis. The truth is all of us here have issues, but our God graciously continues to deal with each of us. We, in turn, can deal with each other in grace and love. We live, move, breath, and backfloat in grace here, and it is glorious. We were once dead in our sins but are now alive to God, having been made alive by Him. His grace has saved us solely because of His mercy and not because of anything we have done. We cannot help but speak and testify of what He has done for us and what He has taught us. We have hard times, but our troubles drive us closer to the God we all love and to each other. We pray that the words of our mouth and the meditation of our hearts are pleasing to God. We hope this book will motivate and inspire you to praise and glorify God with us for His goodness, mercy, and grace.

My mother also wrote this book for anyone who has ever been to our home. If you have shared a meal with us, you have become one of our people. We love you and are daily praying that God will draw you closer to Himself. If, through the sovereignty of God, you are holding this book and we have never met you before, we are also praying for you. We pray that you would learn how to abide with God personally, with your family, and in a church where you can worship God together with other believers. We are praying that God would be your main thing.

We firmly believe that the Gospel – the death, burial, and resurrection of Jesus Christ – has saved us. "Neither is there salvation in any other: for there is none other name under heaven given among men, whereby we must be saved." (Acts 4:12) We summon you to believe in Him and enter into the kingdom of God. If you already believe, we invite you into a closer relationship with God by abiding with Him.

We know Who we have believed, and we are persuaded that He is able to keep what we have committed to Him against the final day (2 Timothy 1:12). We know that our Redeemer lives, and that He will stand on the earth (Job 19:25). We believe the times are ripe for a new reformation, a new revival within the church today the likes of which the earth has never seen. And we believe this revival will come when individuals, families, churches, and nations abide with God.

All praise, honor, and glory be to our great God, Father, Son, and Holy Spirit, world without end, and Amen. We really love You, God.

Joseph Pates
Son and Editor

CHAPTER 1

What is the main thing?

• • •

*"For Christ also hath once suffered for
sins, the just for the unjust, that he might
bring us to God, being put to death in the
flesh, but quickened by the Spirit."*

1 PETER 3:18

THE MAIN THING IN LIFE is God. We were created to know
God and enjoy Him. We should strive to constantly abide
in Him by doing everything with Him and for His glory.
Walking with God personally and corporately helps us abide
with God in every area of life. Knowing God through the
enjoyment of having a close personal relationship with Him
should be the ultimate priority, the starting point, the end
goal, the foundation, and the center of every true Christian's
life every day. This makes God your God, not just the God
of your parents or the God of your church or the God of
the universe. The main thing in life is to know, enjoy, walk
with, and abide with your God.

Who is the One True God? We would never know unless He revealed Himself to us. The wonderful news is that He has! Through the Bible, God's Word for us, we can meet God, enter into a personal relationship with Him, and grow to know Him more and more.

Moses asked God to show Himself to him. "And [God] said, I will make all my goodness pass before thee, and I will proclaim the name of the Lord before thee; and will be gracious to whom I will be gracious, and will shew mercy on whom I will shew mercy" (Exodus 33:19). God then revealed Himself to Moses, proclaiming that He was "The Lord, The Lord God, merciful and gracious, longsuffering, and abundant in goodness and truth, keeping mercy for thousands, forgiving iniquity and transgression and sin" (Exodus 34:6-7).

God wants to be known and initiates our relationship with Him. John 6:44 says, "No man can come to me, except the Father which hath sent me draw him." We will only want a relationship with the true and living God because He draws us to Himself. 1 John 4:19 says, "We love him, because he first loved us." God initiates. God pursues. God seeks and saves the lost. "According as he hath chosen us in him before the foundation of the world, that we should be holy and without blame before him in love" (Ephesians 1:4). "Not by works of righteousness which we have done, but according to his mercy he saved us, by the washing of regeneration, and renewing of the Holy Ghost" (Titus 3:5). Apart from God's amazing grace to us, we could never enter into a relationship with God. Romans 3:10-11 states, "As it is written, There is none righteous, no, not one: There is none that understandeth, there is none that seeketh after God." Ephesians 2:8 says, "For by grace are ye saved through faith; and that not of yourselves: it is the gift of God."

1 Peter 3:18 tells us that the reason why Jesus Christ suffered and died for us is to bring us near to God. Jesus died for us so we could have a saving relationship with Him. But this relationship doesn't just get us out of hell and into heaven. It brings us close to God right now. Deuteronomy 30:19-20 says, "I have set before you life and death, blessing and cursing: therefore choose life, that both thou and thy seed may live: That thou mayest love the Lord thy God, and that thou mayest obey his voice, and that thou mayest cleave unto him: for he is thy life . . . ."

CHAPTER 2

Why did God create us?

• • •

"Thou art worthy, O Lord, to receive glory and honour and power: for thou hast created all things, and for thy pleasure they are and were created."

REVELATION 4:11

WHY DID GOD CREATE US? Having a relationship with God brings Him pleasure. The reason God saves us is not merely to take us to heaven when we die. 1 Peter 3:18 says, "For Christ also hath once suffered for sins, the just for the unjust, that he might bring us to God." Being brought near to God is the goal. God wants us to know Him. God wants us to enter into a relationship with Him now that will continue throughout all eternity.

Once God saves us, we are made new. "Seeing that ye have put off the old man with his deeds; And have put on the new man, which is renewed in knowledge after the image of him that created him" (Colossians 3:9-10). We were created in the image of God, which means we are like Him and can enter into a relationship with Him. Our sin prevented us from having a relationship with God, but all Christians have been regenerated from death to life by the Holy Spirit made manifest to us by God's saving grace alone. 1 Corinthians 3:16 says, "Know ye not that ye are the temple of God, and that the Spirit of God dwelleth in you?" Romans 8:9-11 says, "But ye are not in the flesh, but in the Spirit, if so be that the Spirit of God dwell in you. Now if any man have not the Spirit of Christ, he is none of his. And if Christ be in you, the body is dead because of sin; but the Spirit is life because of righteousness. But if the Spirit of him that raised up Jesus from the dead dwell in you, he that raised up Christ from the dead shall also quicken your mortal bodies by his Spirit that dwelleth in you." When God saves us, He quickens us by His Holy Spirit to respond to Him. When God quickens us, He brings us from death to life. Once we have been quickened, we want a relationship with God. We repent. We respond. We believe.

Once we have been made alive in Christ by the power of the Holy Spirit, we have a new desire to know God. Deuteronomy 4:29 says, "But if from thence thou shalt seek the Lord thy God, thou shalt find him, if thou seek him with all thy heart and with all thy soul." Once we are brought into a saving relationship with God, seeking Him should be our main thing. Knowing God, desiring God, enjoying God, communicating with God, and worshipping God should be the goal of our life everyday. The one true and living God wants us to know Him, be in fellowship with Him, talk to Him, and do everything with Him and for His glory. The Bible often describes this way of living as walking with God. As you walk with God in everything you do, you are in a sense living in heaven right here on earth. We do not have to wait for heaven to know God and enjoy Him. It is the reason why we exist, and it brings God pleasure. Seeking to know God and enjoy Him should be the main thing that we pursue everyday.

CHAPTER 3

Who is the God of the Bible?

• • •

"For there are three that bear record in heaven, the Father, the Word, and the Holy Ghost: and these three are one."

1 JOHN 5:7

THE ONE TRUE GOD OF the Bible has made Himself known to us. He is triune in nature. He is one God who exists in three Persons: God the Father, God the Son Jesus, and God the Holy Spirit. We primarily see the Trinity by looking at Scripture as a whole. The three Persons in the Godhead are all equal in power, glory, and perfection. They differ in function, but they are all perfect in holiness, love, justice, grace, mercy, goodness, patience, kindness, faithfulness, and truth. All three Persons are eternal, infinite, immutable, omniscient, wise, omnipotent, transcendent, and omnipresent.

This Three-in-One God has existed in a perfect relationship of love and joy for all of eternity. Praying for His Church, Jesus asked the Father to unite His people as one "even as we are one: I in them, and thou in me . . . that the world may know that thou hast sent me, and hast loved them, as thou hast loved me" (John 17:22-23). This relational God has created people to enter into the fellowship of a relationship with Him. God's desire for the Church as a whole, and therefore for each one of us individually, is that we all become partakers of the everlasting love between God the Father and God the Son. This occurs in us because of the work of the Holy Spirit.

Because God is eternal, all of His attributes are eternal. We will be getting to know God and building our relationship with Him forever. God is infinite. Therefore, God is the only one who is able to completely satisfy the desire we all have to be in a love relationship with someone that will never end. A relationship with God will never disappoint us and can completely satisfy every desire of our hearts. Knowing God more intimately will strengthen our relationship with Him, bolster our faith in Him, and help us understand what He has been doing throughout human history.

CHAPTER 4

What has God been doing throughout human history?

• • •

*"For God so loved the world, that he gave
his only begotten Son, that whosoever
believeth in him should not perish, but have
everlasting life. For God sent not his Son
into the world to condemn the world; but that
the world through him might be saved."*

JOHN 3:16-17

WHAT HAS GOD BEEN DOING throughout human history? God
is writing the greatest story ever told as He directs history
through His providence and sovereignty. It is a story of a
God who has been in a loving relationship between Father,
Son, and Spirit throughout eternity past and a God who created people to enter into this relationship.

All throughout the Old Testament, we read of covenants.
God initiates and establishes covenants with His people and

guarantees them by His Word. Through the many covenants in the Bible, we see that God wants to walk with His people and have a covenantal relationship with them.

In the Garden of Eden, God walked with Adam and Eve. God made a covenant of life with Adam and Eve. Sin entered the world through Adam and Eve's disobedience to the covenant of life, and then they hid from God. Although Adam and Eve's disobedience to God's command not to eat of the tree of knowledge of good and evil was indicative of many different sins, Adam and Eve were ultimately declaring by eating the fruit that they did not love and trust God completely. By sinning against God, they were choosing to walk alone. However, God pursued them, found them, and promised them a Redeemer who would pay for their sin (Genesis 3:15).

Despite the curse of sin, God still pursued the people He had created and desired them to walk with Him. Enoch walked with God, and he was no more. Walking with God is heaven on earth. God took Enoch to heaven where he is still walking with God in eternal bliss.

Noah walked with God and found grace in the eyes of the Lord. God established a covenant with Noah and kept him safe in the Ark.

God made a covenant with Abraham by promising him children, land, and blessing upon the nations through His Seed. Abraham had a wonderful relationship with God because he believed God and walked with Him. Abraham was called God's friend and talked with Him as a friend.

Friendship is an intimate relationship. Amazingly, this is the kind of intimate, close, and personal relationship God wants to have with us.

God made a covenant with Moses and told him how His people should walk with Him and relate to Him through obedience to the laws God established. The law shows us that we should be holy because God is holy. The problem is that we are not holy. The Bible calls this lack of holiness and perfection "sin." God's people continued to fall short of God's perfect standard over the many centuries that followed, but God continued to promise a future Savior.

Why would God require perfection and give us commands we cannot possibly keep? He wanted us to know we needed a relationship with someone who is perfect and therefore could rescue and save us from our sins. We need a relationship with the perfect God-man, Jesus. The Bible tells us Jesus is completely God (John 1:1) and therefore perfectly holy. He is infinite and therefore capable to bridge the infinite divide between God's holiness and our complete sinfulness. However, Jesus was also completely human (John 1:14). Jesus became a man when God the Holy Spirit placed Him in the womb of the virgin Mary. Jesus was born of her without sin and lived a perfectly sinless life.

"Ye shall be holy: for I the Lord your God am holy" (Leviticus 19:2). The problem is that we are not holy, and we all know it. "If we say that we have no sin, we deceive ourselves, and the truth is not in us" (1 John 1:8). "For all have sinned, and come short of the glory of God" (Romans

3:23). The Bible defines sin in 1 John 5:17: "All unrighteousness is sin." 1 John 3:4 says, "Sin is the transgression of the law." James 4:17 says, "Therefore to him that knoweth to do good, and doeth it not, to him it is sin." Because we all know we have sinned, we all know we are unworthy of this personal relationship that the One True Holy God seeks to have with us. Isaiah 59:2 tells us, "But your iniquities have separated between you and your God, and your sins have hid his face from you, that he will not hear." Unless God seeks us and saves us, we will die and be utterly lost. Romans 6:23 says, "For the wages of sin is death; but the gift of God is eternal life through Jesus Christ our Lord." The consequence for sin is death and complete separation from God eternally. Luke 19:10 tells us the good news: "For the Son of man is come to seek and to save that which was lost."

CHAPTER 5

What is the Gospel?

• • •

"Moreover, brethren, I declare unto you the gospel which I preached unto you, which also ye have received, and wherein ye stand; By which also ye are saved, if ye keep in memory what I preached unto you, unless ye have believed in vain. For I delivered unto you first of all that which I also received, how that Christ died for our sins according to the scriptures; And that he was buried, and that he rose again the third day according to the scriptures."

1 Corinthians 15:1-4

THE GOSPEL IS THE DEATH, burial, and resurrection of Jesus Christ. This is the greatest event in all of human history. Jesus assumed the body of a man, lived a perfect life, died on the cross to pay for our sins, was buried, and rose from the dead to give us eternal life.

Why did Jesus have to die? The Bible tells us that sin separates us from God (Isaiah 59:2). Romans 6:23 says, "For the wages of sin is death." Hebrews 9:22 says, "Without shedding of blood is no remission." Leviticus 17:11 shows us that life is found in the blood, and it is blood that makes atonement for the soul. The punishment for our sins is death. Jesus had to give His life and shed His blood to atone and pay for our sin. Because God is perfectly just and holy, sin had to be dealt with. Jesus was the only one who could deal with sin properly. Through the sacrifice of Jesus, God satisfied His perfect justice and became our justifier when Jesus satisfied the wrath of God and paid the penalty for our sin. Through faith in the finished work of Jesus on the cross, we are justified. We are declared legally righteous because all of our sins have been paid for through the death and shed blood of Jesus.

Referring to Jesus, Acts 4:12 says, "...for there is none other name under heaven given among men, whereby we must be saved." We cannot find salvation anywhere or in anyone else. Anyone who believes in what Jesus has done on his or her behalf and asks God to save them will be saved. Romans 10:9 says, "That if thou shalt confess with thy mouth the Lord Jesus, and shalt believe in thine heart that God hath raised him from the dead, thou shalt be saved."

Even though our sins have been paid for, we continue to sin. We are incapable of changing our own hearts and leading sinless lives apart from Christ. After Jesus saves us, He begins the process of sanctification in which He helps us die to sin in our lives and live more righteously. We continue to repent of sin but not in order to be forgiven. After all, we were completely forgiven when Jesus died on the cross and paid for our sins, which happened before we were even born. Rather, we repent to agree with God about our sin, turn from it, and re-enter fellowship with God. Sin hurts all our relationships and especially our relationship with God. He is grieved when we sin. Speaking to God's people, Isaiah says, "But your iniquities have separated between you and your God, and your sins have hid his face from you, that he will not hear" (Isaiah 59:2). We repent to restore the peace and joy of sweet fellowship with God. "If we confess our sins, he is faithful and just to forgive us our sins, and to cleanse us from all unrighteousness" (1 John 1:9). Sin steals, kills, and destroys that fellowship.

Jesus is now sitting at the right hand of God the Father ruling, reigning, and drawing people, families, and nations into a saving relationship with Him. God's sovereign plan from the beginning was to send Jesus, His Son, to make a way for sinful people to have a relationship with Himself.

CHAPTER 6

Why should we be thankful?

• • •

"Rejoice evermore. Pray without ceasing. In every thing give thanks: for this is the will of God in Christ Jesus concerning you."

1 THESSALONIANS 5:16-18

THE MOST IMPORTANT EVENT IN all of human history is the Gospel – the death, burial, and resurrection of Jesus Christ for us. We should be filled with immense gratitude when we realize that Jesus died on the cross, was buried, and rose again *for us.*

Christians should immerse themselves in the Gospel everyday. Remembering that we are sinners who deserve death and complete separation from God in hell should help us not to develop a sense of entitlement. The only thing we are entitled to is death and the pains of hell forever. We do not deserve health, wealth, a pain-free life, perfect relationships, obedient children, or any other bless-ing. God is under no obligation to give us everything we think we need in order to be happy. The truth is that God is all we need to be truly happy. Even though we all deserve hell, God came to rescue and save us because He is merci-ful and full of grace. Remembering what God did for us by sending Jesus into this sinful world to be mocked, beat-en, rejected, spit on, scourged, and whipped should cause our every prayer to Him to be saturated with thanksgiving. He rescued us, He redeemed us, and He made a way for us to know Him. Knowing Jesus died the most humiliating, shameful, and painful death possible for us should cause all of us to burst forth in praise and ceaseless gratitude.

Humiliation and pain were not the cause of His deepest agony. For the first time, the last time, and the only time, Jesus was separated from His Father. When He became sin for us on the cross (2 Corinthians 5:21), Jesus endured the righteous wrath of our Holy God against sin. "Much more then, being now justified by his blood, we shall be saved from wrath through him" (Romans 5:9). God hates sin. We must never forget that we would have had to endure the pain of ultimate separation from God and all good things were it not for Jesus's sacrifice. How can we not respond with gratitude in light of what He has done for us?

Romans 8:32 says, "He that spared not his own Son, but delivered him up for us all, how shall he not with him also freely give us all things?" God is the giver of all good things. James 1:17 says, "Every good and every perfect gift is from above, and cometh down from the Father of lights, with whom is no variableness, neither shadow of turning." Since every good thing comes from God, we should thank Him for it. 1 Thessalonians 5:16-18 says, "Rejoice evermore. Pray without ceasing. In every thing give thanks: for this is the will of God in Christ Jesus concerning you." We should develop the practice of thanking God for the big things, the little things, the hard things, and for everything. Dedicating a part of your prayer time to thanksgiving or keeping a thankfulness journal can help cultivate a thankful spirit.

God is the source of life, love, and joy. He is the giver of life. He is the one who established marriages and families. He is the one who builds our homes and establishes the work of our hands. No relationship, no work, nothing we do apart from God will last. "Except the Lord build the house, they labor in vain that build it" (Psalm 127:1). Everything is meaningless apart from God according to Ecclesiastes. God brings meaning to our work and to our relationships. He is the giver of pleasure and all things that are good. We are completely surrounded with the goodness of God. As Psalm 136:1-3 says, "O give thanks unto the Lord; for he is good: for his mercy endureth for ever. O give thanks unto the God of gods: for his mercy endureth for ever. O give thanks to the Lord of lords: for his mercy endureth for ever."

CHAPTER 7

What is the main point of our existence?

• • •

"He hath shewed thee, O man, what is good; and what doth the Lord require of thee, but to do justly, and to love mercy, and to walk humbly with thy God?"

MICAH 6:8

WHAT IS THE MAIN POINT of our existence? Why are we alive? Why were we born? God wants us to enjoy having a relationship with Him. God, who has existed in perfect love, unity, and fellowship since before time began, has created us to be part of that fellowship, unity, and love. God wants a relationship with us. God wants us to walk with Him.

Relationships are for enjoyment, edification, honoring, cherishing, co-laboring, and loving. Our relationship with God is no different. God wants us to enjoy Him. We enjoy God by spending time with Him. We spend time with

God when we read His Word, talk to Him in prayer, and go to church and worship Him in spirit and in truth with other believers. God wants our whole selves involved in and participating in our relationship with Him. He wants our hearts, souls, and minds engaged as we spend time with Him. We are to offer ourselves as a living sacrifice, holy and acceptable to God (Romans 12:1).

How can we establish or maintain a relationship with a holy God? We can't do it by ourselves. Luke 18:27 says, "The things which are impossible with men are possible with God." God saves us. We can't save ourselves. God initiates our relationship with Him. We respond by crying out to Him for salvation. Hebrews 12:2 identifies Jesus as "the author and finisher of our faith." God starts it, and God will finish it. God also is the one who sanctifies and perfects our faith. Our hearts are desperately wicked and deceitful. We cannot change our hearts, but God can.

Ask God to give you a desire to spend time with Him. We spend time with God when we read our Bibles, pray, sing, listen, worship, sit in silence, fast, and behold His handiwork in nature. When we do all these things with Him, we get to know Him more intimately and come to an understanding of what He is doing.

Life is not about us. It is about God. History is His story and not ours. We are a part of God's story, but not the main point of it. Psalm 115:1 says, "Not unto us, O Lord, not unto us, but unto thy name give glory, for thy mercy, and for thy truth's sake." God, through His providence and sovereignty, is directing all of human history, every person, every event, and every dust particle to accomplish His sovereign will. God is accomplishing the salvation of the world. God told Jesus that He would give Him the nations for His inheritance in Psalm 2. Jesus told His disciples to go into all the world baptizing in the name of the Father, the Son, and the Holy Spirit in Matthew 28. John 3:16 tells us that God so loved the world.

Practically speaking, this means God is ultimately using us to fulfill His sovereign will and plan in this world. That ultimate purpose transcends our little lives and our little problems. This also means that everything we receive in life from God is part of His plan for us. When we whine, complain, or have a bad attitude, we are committing serious sins. We don't tend to think of them this way, but we need to. When we engage in these sins, we are breaking the first commandment and displaying the root of all other sins: pride. We are essentially telling God that if we were our own god, we would not order the events of life the way He has. We are saying it would be better if we were God. We all do it almost every day. We are in high rebellion against God when we feel and act this way. We may think we are justified in having a bad attitude because it is raining and we wanted to go to the beach. But, what we are actually telling the Creator of heaven and earth is that He is not doing a good job ruling and reigning. Instead, we should submit joyfully to every circumstance and situation we find ourselves in by reminding ourselves that God is in control.

We need to learn "in whatsoever state I am, therewith to be content" (Philippians 4:11). We must agree with Job: "… the Lord gave, and the Lord hath taken away; blessed be the name of the Lord" (Job 1:21).

God providentially rules this earth through the laws of nature, circumstances outside of our control, and the authorities He has placed in our lives. It is God's will for you to joyfully submit to and obey your parents, your government, your church leadership, your bosses, and any other authorities He has placed over you (as long as these authorities do not ask you to break His laws). We can either live in rebellion against God all our days, or we can participate joyfully in all that God is doing. We exist as part of God's story, not our own.

CHAPTER 8

How do we walk with God?

• • •

Personally: "For whosoever shall call upon the name of the Lord shall be saved."

ROMANS 10:13

As a Family: "And thou shalt teach them diligently unto thy children, and shalt talk of them when thou sittest in thine house, and when thou walkest by the way, and when thou liest down, and when thou risest up."

DEUTERONOMY 6:7

Corporately: "Not forsaking the assembling of ourselves together, as the manner of some is; but exhorting one another: and so much the more, as ye see the day approaching."

HEBREWS 10:25

GOD ESTABLISHES AN INTIMATE RELATIONSHIP with us as we walk with Him on three levels. Each Christian is an individual person, a member of a family, and should be a member or adherent of a church. This means we must walk with God personally and we must walk with Him corporately within the groups of people (family and church) He has placed us in. Walking with God personally, as a family, and corporately with fellow believers in the Body of Christ deepens our relationship with Him.

Each person created by God must respond to Him personally. People either rebel against God or enter into a relationship of love with Him. Being born into a Christian family does not establish your own relationship with God. If anyone wants a relationship with God, that person must cry out to God themselves. If you want God to save you, you must ask Him. Your parents can't do it for you. If you want to know God, you must seek Him. You must talk to Him yourself in prayer. You must read His Word for yourself. You must direct your affections toward Him. You must prepare your own heart to worship Him each Lord's Day. You must make Him your priority. You must walk with Him. This has to be a personal commitment. You must love the Lord *your* God with all *your* heart, all *your* soul, and all *your* strength (Deuteronomy 6:5, emphasis mine). This is not a call to a selfish, self-focused, and individualistic faith journey but rather to a mere recognition and application of the fact that each of us must abide with God and walk with Him individually. He has saved *you,* so *you* should abide with Him personally. Our personal relationship with God is really a covenantal relationship because He initiates it, perfects it, and will complete it. He makes specific promises to us that we can count on. As believers walking in a personal covenantal relationship with God, we know that He will keep all his promises to us regarding our salvation and sanctification. We can then demonstrate our love for Him in return through faithful obedience (John 14:15).

Your personal relationship with God also has corporate ramifications that cannot be ignored. God has placed all of us in families either as a member of that family or a leader of that family. This means a Christian family must walk with God as a family as well. Doing devotions together, praying together, reading the Bible together, and worshipping God together will knit Christian families closer to God and to each other. Christian families should be distinctively Christian. Deuteronomy 6 commands parents to teach their children how to walk with God. Parents must be constantly teaching their children how to walk with God when they rise in the morning, when they walk by the way, and when they lie down at night (Deuteronomy 6:6-9).

The church is far more than simply the building we go to every Sunday. It is the Kingdom of God, the Body of Christ, and the gathering together of God's people. Hebrews 10:25 tells us that Christians should not forsake the assembly of God's people in corporate worship on the Lord's Day. We have been called and summoned to worship God with a body of believers each Lord's Day. Covenantal renewal worship, the reading and preaching of the Word of God, Psalm and hymn singing, and the partaking of the Lord's Supper strengthens, builds, and accomplishes the sanctification of God's people. There is a real sense in which every time we worship God together with all His people, we are coming into the throne room of God in heaven and to Jesus, the mediator of the new covenant (Hebrews 12:22-24). As we participate in the worship service and fellowship with other believers, we are walking with God corporately.

Walking with God individually, as a family, and corporately with other believers deepens our relationship with God. It is important for all Christians to walk with God in all of these spheres. Walking with God on all of these levels is important to your own spiritual well-being and, if you are a parent, to the spiritual well-being of your children.

CHAPTER 9

How do we glorify God?

• • •

"Among the gods there is none like unto thee,
O Lord; neither are there any works like unto
thy works. All nations whom thou hast made
shall come and worship before thee, O Lord;
and shall glorify thy name. For thou art great,
and doest wondrous things: thou art God alone.
Teach me thy way, O Lord; I will walk in thy
truth: unite my heart to fear thy name. I will
praise thee, O Lord my God, with all my heart:
and I will glorify thy name for evermore."

PSALM 86:8-12

ALL RELATIONSHIPS ARE BUILT WHEN one person gives honor, respect, and love to another. As we glorify and honor God and declare our love for Him, He teaches and edifies us and declares His love for us through His Word and Spirit. Our relationship with Him is thereby strengthened.

No one is more worthy to receive honor and praise than God. He is perfect in all of His work and all of His ways. We glorify God by loving Him and obeying Him. To glorify God, we must love God. We must set our heart's affection on Him, desire Him above all else, and make Him our treasure and our heart's desire. We should be continually searching our hearts and our lives for things we love and desire more than God. It could be family, friends, money, beauty, fitness, health, power, influence, positions of authority, recognition, justice, a relationship, marriage, a baby, a house, a car, a job, a degree, food, obedient children, a pain-free life, or many other things. A thousand things everyday are competing with God to be our first love. We must have no other loves before our love for God. He should be our first love. God should be all we need to be happy. God is more than enough to satisfy every desire of our hearts. If you don't believe this, you either believe a lie or you really don't know the one true God of the Bible. He is unimaginably awesome, beautiful, great, mighty, and completely worthy of all the glory we could ever give Him.

Jesus said that if we love Him, we will do what He commands. Obedience without love is meaningless, but true love should lead to true heartfelt obedience. Obedience is doing what we are told, right away, with a happy spirit. We can only truly obey God through the help of the Holy Spirit, and we will only obey Him if we love Him.

What does God command? You must read the entire Bible to know every one of God's commands. God summarized His commands for Moses and the Israelites in Exodus 20, the Ten Commandments. Jesus summarized them further for us in Matthew 22:36-40: "Thou shalt love the Lord thy God with all thy heart, and with all thy soul, and with all thy mind. This is the first and great commandment. And the second is like unto it, Thou shalt love thy neighbor as thyself. On these two commandments hang all the law and the prophets." Paul summarized it even further in Romans 13:10 where it says, "Love worketh no ill to his neighbor: therefore love is the fulfilling of the law."

Another way of saying this is that God ultimately commands us to believe and love. "And this is his commandment, That we should believe on the name of his Son Jesus Christ, and love one another, as he gave us commandment" (1 John 3:23). What does it mean to believe? Biblically speaking, believing is action. When we believe, we act a certain way. What does God want us to believe? He wants us to believe that He exists, that He created the world, that He is triune in nature, that His Gospel is actually accomplishing salvation, and that He will keep all of His promises. What does God promise? He promises to love us, guide us, comfort us, send the Holy Spirit, answer prayer, and save us, among many other things. Apart from God, we are incapable of the ability to believe. Philippians 1:29 says, "For unto you it is given in the behalf of Christ, not only to believe on him, but also to suffer for his sake." Ask, and you will receive (Matthew 7:7).

God defines biblical love in many places in Scripture. "Love is patient, love is kind. It does not envy, it does not boast, it is not proud. It does not dishonor others, it is not self-seeking, it is not easily angered, it keeps no record of wrongs. Love does not delight in evil but rejoices with the truth. It always protects, always trusts, always hopes, always perseveres. Love never fails" (1 Corinthians 13:4-8 NIV). Biblical love is action. In John 3:16 it says, "For God so loved the world, that he *gave* his only begotten Son . . . " (emphasis mine). God loved us by giving us Jesus. John 15:13 says biblical love is sacrificial actions: "Greater love hath no man than this, that a man lay down his life for his friends." The greatest act of love in all of human history is when Jesus died on the cross for us. He laid down His life for us. Apart from God, we are incapable of loving God or our neighbor with true biblical sacrificial love. Praise the Lord that Jesus was not just a teacher! Jesus is our Savior. When He saves us, He indwells us. He changes our hearts. He sanctifies us. He redeems us. He helps us do what we cannot do no matter how hard we try. We cannot love God or our neighbor, but Christ in us can.

We do not get to write our own story. God is writing our story. 1 Corinthians 6:19-20 says, "What? know ye not that your body is the temple of the Holy Ghost which is in you, which ye have of God, and ye are not your own? For ye are bought with a price: therefore glorify God in your body, and in your spirit, which are God's." By completely laying down our wants, desires, goals, ambitions, and plans through joyful submission to God within the circumstances we find ourselves in, we will find our lives. Jesus said in Matthew 16:24-25, "If any man will come after me, let him deny himself, and take up his cross, and follow me. For whosoever will save his life shall lose it: and whosoever will lose his life for my sake shall find it." Psalm 47:4 says that God chooses our inheritance for us. When we want God's will His way, we find true rest. God will fight for us. Philippians 1:6 says God will complete the good work He started in us. We need only wait and see what God will do for us. 1 Corinthians 2:9 says, "But as it is written, Eye hath not seen, nor ear heard, neither have entered into the heart of man, the things which God hath prepared for them that love him." Not only should we be laying down our lives in complete surrender to God, we should be laying down our lives for others. We die so that we can truly live. In Christ, death is always followed by a resurrection to new life. God is glorified in us when we die to ourselves and live for Him and for others.

CHAPTER 10

Why should we read the Bible and pray?

• • •

*"With my whole heart have I sought thee: O let
me not wander from thy commandments. Thy
word have I hid in mine heart, that I might not
sin against thee. Blessed art thou, O Lord: teach
me thy statutes. With my lips have I declared
all the judgments of thy mouth. I have rejoiced
in the way of thy testimonies, as much as in
all riches. I will meditate in thy precepts, and
have respect unto thy ways. I will delight myself
in thy statutes: I will not forget thy word."*

Psalm 119:10-16

"Pray without ceasing."

1 Thessalonians 5:17

ALL TRUE CHRISTIANS SHOULD DAILY take time to read the Bible, which is the Word of God, and talk to God in prayer. Christians who read the Bible and pray every day will be spiritually nourished and equipped for every good work the Lord places in front of them to do. They will also be equipped to share the Gospel if anyone asks about the hope that is within them (1 Peter 3:15).

The Bible is the inspired Word of God. We should read the Word of God on a daily basis, so we can know God more intimately. The more we know God, the deeper and more intimate our relationship with Him will be. As we learn the promises of God for us in His Word, we grow in our trust of Him. All relationships are built on trust, and our relationship with God is no different. The more we read about His promises, His nature, His purpose, His plan, His incredible love for us, and what He has done on our behalf, the more we will love and trust Him.

Bible reading should be a top priority in the life of a true Christian. Reading the Bible strengthens our faith and ability to trust God. The Bible says, "But without faith it is impossible to please him . . . " (Hebrews 11:6). Romans 10:17 says, "...faith cometh by hearing, and hearing by the word of God." We seek God by immersing ourselves in Scripture. God says that when we seek Him, He will allow us to find Him. Deuteronomy 4:29 says, "But if from thence thou shalt seek the Lord thy God, thou shalt find him, if thou seek him with all thy heart and with all thy soul." This is truly amazing! The Almighty God will allow us to know Him if we seek Him with all our hearts. As we read our Bibles, we come to love God more and know Him more intimately.

True Christians should want to know everything God has said. We should want to read through the entire Bible. It helps tremendously to have a plan. If you want to have a relationship with someone, you must listen to them and spend time with them. Reading the Bible is how we listen to God. Listening to the Word of God is another wonderful way to spend time with God. You can purchase the Bible on CD or DVD. You can also find Bible audio programs online with recordings for each day of the year. Listening to the Word of God this way builds our faith and strengthens our relationship with God.

Continually reviewing God's story from Genesis to Revelation is a wonderful way to see God's message as a whole. Orally reading the same passages over and over in some regular pattern is a wonderful way to memorize the Bible. It helps your tongue speak God's word, which makes sharing your faith with the very words of Scripture easy and natural because you have practiced. It also helps you re-member where these passages are in the Bible for quick and easy referencing.

The more you read the Bible, listen to it, and recite it, the more you will love it! These words will get into your head, your mouth, and your heart, and they will change your life. Jesus said in Matthew 4:4, "Man shall not live by bread alone, but by every word that proceedeth out of the mouth of God." The Bible is our spiritual food. We should be feasting on it everyday. The more we love it, the more we will be excited to share it with our children and with others. How wonderful it would be if we could say about our children what Paul said about Timothy in 2 Timothy 3:15-17! "And that from a child thou hast known the holy scriptures, which are able to make thee wise unto salvation through faith which is in Christ Jesus. All scripture is given by inspiration of God, and is profitable for doctrine, for reproof, for correction, for instruction in righteousness: That the man of God may be perfect, thoroughly furnished unto all good works." The words of God should be the main words that fill our hearts and minds and the hearts and minds of our children. "Set your hearts unto all the words which I testify among you this day, which ye shall command your children to observe to do, all the words of this law. For it is not a vain thing for you; because it is your life: and through this thing ye shall prolong your days in the land . . ." (Deuteronomy 32:46-47).

Prayer is talking to God. We are commanded in Scripture to pray "without ceasing" (1 Thessalonians 5:17). This verse alone should be motivation for us to cultivate and develop a meaningful prayer time with God. Many people do not know how to pray. Jesus provided the Lord's Prayer specifically for this reason. "After this manner therefore pray ye: Our Father which art in heaven, Hallowed be thy name.

Thy kingdom come, Thy will be done in earth, as it is in heaven. Give us this day our daily bread. And forgive us our debts, as we forgive our debtors. And lead us not into temptation, but deliver us from evil: For thine is the kingdom, and the power, and the glory, for ever. Amen" (Matthew 6:9-13). Many resources exist to help Christians focus their hearts and minds on God and on His Word during prayer. It is worth your while to invest in whatever tools you feel are necessary to develop the spiritual discipline of talking to God in meaningful prayer. You can pray silently, out loud, or write your prayers in a journal. All of these activities are beneficial.

Remember that your Father already knows what you need before you ask Him (Matthew 6:8). We pray first and foremost to deepen our relationship with God. We pray to understand His will for us from His Word and from His Holy Spirit, so this will continually change the way we pray. Prayer changes us also. "Be careful for nothing; but in every thing by prayer and supplication with thanksgiving let your requests be made known unto God. And the peace of God, which passeth all understanding, shall keep your hearts and minds through Christ Jesus" (Philippians 4:6-7) When we pray, the Holy Spirit fills us with peace and guards our hearts and minds. We are changed. The peace of the Holy Spirit that we receive through prayer gives us the ability to love difficult people and endure hard providences.

Starting your prayers by praising God helps you focus your heart and mind on the object of your prayers. "O Lord, our Lord, how excellent is thy name in all the earth! who has set thy glory above the heavens" (Psalm 8:1). God is awesome, and His attributes are worth meditating on in prayer. He is holy, good, kind, righteous, sovereign, merciful, generous, gracious, patient, and just among many other things.

Thanking God in your prayers helps you remember the source of your life and all your blessings. As you thank God in prayer, it will help produce joy and contentment within you. "O give thanks unto the Lord; for he is good: because his mercy endureth for ever" (Psalm 118:1). "In every thing give thanks: for this is the will of God in Christ Jesus concerning you" (1 Thessalonians 5:18).

Daily confessing your sins to God restores your fellowship with God and makes it sweet. "But your iniquities have separated between you and your God, and your sins have hid his face from you, that he will not hear" (Isaiah 59:2). It is important to note that the Holy Spirit spoke these words through Isaiah to the children of God. Immediately before, it states, "…shew *my people* their transgression . . ." (Isaiah 58:1). Christians must constantly engage in confession of sin to restore their sweet fellowship with God. "If we say that we have no sin, we deceive ourselves, and the truth is not in us. If we confess our sins, he is faithful and just to forgive us our sins, and to cleanse us from all unrighteousness" (1 John 1:8-9).

We are also encouraged to bring our needs and the needs of those around us to God in prayer. "Praying always with all prayer and supplication in the Spirit, and watching thereunto with all perseverance and supplication for all saints" (Ephesians 6:18). "Casting all your care upon him; for he careth for you" (1 Peter 5:7). We are encouraged to pray for our leaders and authorities. "I exhort therefore, that, first of all, supplications, prayers, intercessions, and giving of thanks, be made for all men; For kings, and for all that are in authority; that we may lead a quiet and peaceable life in all godliness and honesty" (1 Timothy 2:1-2). Our prayers really do have an impact in the world, even if we do not see it right away. "The effectual fervent prayer of a righteous man availeth much" (James 5:16).

Prayer helps us to discern the will of God. We must remember that, ultimately, we want God to accomplish His will and not ours. When we pray this way, we are following Jesus' example. "And he said, Abba, Father, all things are possible unto thee; take away this cup from me: nevertheless not what I will, but what thou wilt" (Mark 14:36).

All relationships are built by spending time together. Countless Scriptures specifically command or implicitly assume the fact that a thriving follower of God should constantly be spending time in prayer and reading and meditating on the Word of God. "Pray without ceasing" (1 Thessalonians 5:17). "Blessed is the man that walketh not in the counsel of the ungodly, nor standeth in the way of sinners, nor sitteth in the seat of the scornful. But his delight is in the law of the Lord; and in his law doth he meditate day and night" (Psalm 1:1-2). "Thy word have I hid in mine heart, that I might not sin against thee" (Psalm 119:11).

"Thy word is a lamp unto my feet, and a light unto my path" (Psalm 119:105). Furthermore, the Bible tells us that Jesus spent quiet time with His Father. "And in the morning, rising up a great while before day, he went out, and departed into a solitary place, and there prayed" (Mark 1:35). True Christians always want to be like Jesus. Consequently, all believers should set aside a dedicated portion of time each day to spend time with God in Scripture reading and prayer.

CHAPTER 11

Why must we prioritize?

• • •

"For where your treasure is, there
will your heart be also."

MATTHEW 6:21

HOW DO WE KEEP THE main thing the main thing? We must choose to put God first everyday, every week, personally, financially, as a family, in our hearts, in our minds, in our soul, and with all our strength. Prioritizing does not come down to where we spend the greatest amount of our time or what we do the very first thing, although those things can be indicative of what our true priorities are. Prioritizing is ultimately about the orientation of our hearts, our minds, and our souls. On one occasion, someone asked Jesus which commandment was the greatest. Jesus responded, "Thou shalt love the Lord thy God with all thy heart, and with all thy soul, and with all thy mind" (Matthew 22:37).

Christians should personally strive to do everything with God and for His glory. 1 Corinthians 10:31 says, "Whether therefore ye eat, or drink, or whatsoever ye do, do all to the glory of God." Prayer should become one continual conversation with God. 1 Thessalonians 5:17 says, "Pray without ceasing." Our relationship with God should so permeate us that God is one of the first things we think about when we wake up and one of the last things we think about when we lie down to sleep. "My voice shalt thou hear in the morning, O Lord; in the morning will I direct my prayer unto thee, and will look up" (Psalm 5:3). Psalm 63:6-7 says, "I remember thee upon my bed, and meditate on thee in the night watches. Because thou hast been my help, therefore in the shadow of thy wings will I rejoice."

Starting every day with God as your main thing looks different for everyone. On the Lord's Day, spending time with God should involve worship with a body of fellow believers, a gathering we are called not to neglect (Hebrews 10:25). All throughout the week, you can spend time with God by praying, reading and meditating on God's Word, sitting quietly in His presence, listening to music that sets your heart's affection on God, taking a walk with Him, exercising with Him, finding a spot outside to sit with Him and enjoy His creation, writing in your prayer journal to Him, or simply speaking His name as you get out of bed. It does not ultimately matter how you do it or how long it takes. What matters most is that you make God your main thing everyday and then walk with Him throughout your entire day. He will show you what you need to do and help you as you do it. Give God your first and your best. This can take two seconds, five minutes, or two hours. Make walking with God and glorifying Him the top priority in your life and in the life of your family.

Having a personal daily "quiet time" is not absolutely essential to abide with God, but it is a tremendous spiritual discipline to cultivate that helps you read the Word of God and pray on a regular basis. Many people find a daily quiet time is a helpful and even necessary tool to set their hearts and minds on God. Do not think of your walk with God solely in terms of your own "personal" time and relationship with God because that could place less importance on family and corporate worship, and all are important. A daily quiet time is not individualistic because it helps you focus your heart and mind on God and that, in turn, helps you worship God with your family and prepares you to worship in spirit and truth corporately. Actually, you are preparing for the Lord's Day all week through your individual quiet times and family worship. It is important for followers of God to individually read His Word and pray to make their faith their own.

To be a *true* worshipper of God with your family and in your church, you must have a personal saving relationship with God. Otherwise, you are just going through the motions. This is the form of religion but not the substance of true Christianity. A true Christian saved by the power of the Holy Spirit will want to know God and build a relationship with Him personally, with their family, and corporately.

Worshipping God as a family is also important. It helps if you set aside time everyday. Family worship prepares your family to worship God together on the Lord's Day. Husbands and fathers are to obey God by washing their wives with the Word of God and instructing their children in the way they should go (Ephesians 6:4, Proverbs 22:6). This sets a good example for your children. Family worship does not need to be complicated or lengthy. Read the Bible and pray. It will grow as you grow and change as you change. Start simple, but start today. Sometimes it will be short, and other days it will be longer. You will have to fight to establish it, but once you do, you will be eternally gratefully you did not get discouraged and give up on family worship. Nothing brings more meaning to your days than ending them by worshipping the God you love with the people you love most.

Worshipping corporately is the pinnacle of our relationship with God. Corporate worship is what we were made for and what we will be doing throughout all eternity. Every fiber in your being was created to worship God. "For a day in thy courts is better than a thousand" (Psalm 84:10). Don't miss out! Corporate worship is not about you, what you get out of it, how you are feeling, or who you talked to after the service. It is about God. It is His day. We are commanded to honor the Sabbath day and keep it holy (Exodus 20:8). When we obey God and keep the Sabbath day holy by corporately worshipping God, we are transformed, taught, corrected, exhorted, reproved, equipped, fed, strengthened, and encouraged. Our faith is strengthened. We are spiritually fed and nourished by coming to the Lord's table. Corporate worship is accomplishing something in each individual worshipping and in the body of believers as a whole, and it is also accomplishing something in this world. Corporate worship is war. We are taking dominion for the Kingdom of God. When we skip church, we miss out on all of this.

If your life is so busy that you don't have time to keep the main thing the main thing personally, as a family, or corporately, ask God to give you wisdom and help you reprioritize. Consider simplifying and eliminating activities if this is necessary for you to make the time you need to abide with God. This may be especially necessary to consider if you have a family. In Matthew 16:26, Jesus said, "For what is a man profited, if he shall gain the whole world, and lose his own soul? or what shall a man give in exchange for his soul?" The souls of our children and their eternal destiny are worth anything we have to give up to teach them how to walk with God personally, as a family, and corporately. This takes a tremendous amount of time and sacrifice. It is worth anything we have to give up to say with John, "I have no greater joy than to hear that my children walk in truth" (3 John 4). In Matthew 5:30, Jesus said, "And if thy right hand offend thee, cut it off, and cast it from thee..." To have a priority-driven lifestyle where you are able to keep the main thing the main thing, you will sometimes have to say no to a lot of good things. This takes wisdom. James 1:5 says, "If any of you lack wisdom, let him ask of God, that giveth to all men liberally, and upbraideth not; and it shall be given him." Jesus is wisdom incarnate according to 1 Corinthians 1:24, where it says that Christ is "the power of God, and the wisdom of God." When you eliminate the busyness that distracts and keep God as your main thing, you will have the wisdom you desire - because you will have more of Jesus!

CHAPTER 12

How do we make personal application?

• • •

"And let us not be weary in well doing: for in due season we shall reap, if we faint not."

GALATIANS 6:9

DON'T GET DISCOURAGED. KEEPING THE main thing the main thing is hard, really hard. It sounds simple, and it is, but it won't be easy. Many things will creep in, pop up, and "need" your immediate attention. You will be tempted to give up, but don't give up! It is worth fighting for. With God's help, you can make the main thing a reality in your life and in the life of your family.

Keeping God as your number one priority is a fight worth fighting. You must do battle with the world, your flesh, the devil, your thoughts, your exhaustion, your schedule, your children's attention, and all the other little and big things that will try to distract you. Keep God first and all the things you need to get done will get done everyday.

Christian children need to be taught how to keep the main thing the main thing in life. It does not come naturally to them or to anyone else. It is a spiritual discipline. They also need to be shown how to prioritize. Parents always lead by example whether they like it or not. Your children will do what you do. However, the main thing is so important that daily instruction and repetition is essential to cement it in their minds. It is shocking to ask children who have grown up in Christian homes questions about what true saving Christianity is all about. Many don't know the key doctrines of the Christian faith. Most children know the "do's and don'ts," but they completely miss the main thing. Christian children need to know that Christianity is enjoying a personal relationship with God by abiding with Him and making Him their heart's desire. It is not about rule keeping. In Matthew 6:21, Jesus said, "For where your treasure is, there will your heart be also." We must teach our children to treasure God and to want and desire Him more than they want or desire anything else. God must be their main thing.

Many applications can be made once God is your number one priority. If God is not your main thing, then something else is. The Bible calls this sin idolatry. Anything, even good things, can become idols in your life. If we have an idol, God will destroy it or give you over to it (Ezekiel 30:13,

Psalm 81:11-12, Romans 1:24). If you think you are doing all the "right" things but it is not resulting in good fruit, it may be because you have an idol in your life. Christianity is not about obeying a list of rules and doing all the "right" things. It is about keeping your relationship with God the main thing. Bringing up our children in the nurture and admonition of the Lord is all about teaching them how to walk with God in a deep, close, personal relationship and not simply teaching them to obey. Children can be taught to be obedient and moral. However, many obedient and moral people are going to hell when they die. We must teach our children the way they should go. We must beg God to save our children by bringing them into a personal covenantal relationship with Himself. Once the Holy Spirit indwells them, they will learn to love God. If they truly love God, they will obey Him. Giving your children a Christian education, homeschooling them, not allowing them to watch television, having them use a courtship model, limiting their access to technology, having high entertainment standards, or dressing them modestly will not "work" or save them if God is not their first love, their treasure, and their heart's desire. However, if God is their first love, all will be well with them and with their souls. Right behavior will also naturally fall into place because they will have a rightly oriented heart. This is true for our children, and it is true for us.

It is imperative that we do not judge others. God calls each person and each family to different callings and ministries.

We must not judge how different families make personal applications. We cannot peer into other people's hearts to see if God is their main thing. Importantly, we must remember we are not called to do that. Only God can make accurate judgments. In Matthew 7:1, Jesus said, "Judge not, that ye be not judged." God calls each of us to different walks with Him, which is glorious! When God is our main thing, we can make life applications as the Holy Spirit guides us and can allow others to do the same thing.

There is no single way to abide with God personally or as a family. Many different options exist for making personal application. Fruit will be the evidence of the true source. In Matthew 7:20, Jesus said, "Wherefore by their fruits ye shall know them." We must remember that fruit takes a long time to grow, so we must be patient with ourselves, our children, and with others. We are called to keep God the main thing personally and in our own family. We are not called to judge others.

We all know there is not enough time to do everything that needs to be done everyday. If we do not do the most important things first, we may never get to them. When we make walking with God the top priority everyday, we have rightly ordered our priorities. In Luke 10, we read the story of Mary and Martha. Martha was upset because she was serving Jesus while Mary was sitting at Jesus' feet listening to Him. Jesus said, "Martha, Martha, thou art careful and troubled about many things: But one thing is needful: and Mary hath chosen that good part, which shall not be taken away from her" (Luke 10:41-42). We can truly rest when God is our main thing because it is God who is at work in us to will and to do His good pleasure.

Sitting at Jesus' feet, listening to His words, and enjoying time with Him personally, as a family, and in the worship of the church should characterize our relationship with God. All of our life, not just our personal quiet times and our Lord's Day worship, should be devoted to abiding with God as we live the life He has called us to live. This is a deeply spiritual endeavor because the Holy Spirit is indwelling us. Jesus said, "If a man love me, he will keep my words: and my Father will love him, and we will come unto him, and make our abode with him" (John 14:23). This verse is fulfilled in the work of the Holy Spirit. Days will come where we do not feel close to God. However, if we truly are believers in Jesus, God the Holy Spirit Himself is indwelling us all the time whether we "feel" like He is there or not. It is crucially important that we believe the Word of God and not our feelings on any given day. If we do not feel close to God, this should motivate us to pray and see if we, and not God, are the problem. "Search me, O God, and know my heart: try me, and know my thoughts: And see if there be any wicked way in me, and lead me in the way everlasting" (Psalm 139:23-24). "Draw nigh to God, and he will draw nigh to you" (James 4:8). If you truly seek God with all your heart, you will find Him (Jeremiah 29:13).

CHAPTER 13

Why keep the main thing the main thing?

• • •

"But seek ye first the kingdom of God,
and his righteousness; and all these
things shall be added unto you."

MATTHEW 6:33

WHY SHOULD WE KEEP THE main thing the main thing? Should we keep the main thing the main thing just because doing things God's way is better then doing things the world's way? Should we keep the main thing the main thing because it works? Should we keep the main thing the main thing just so we will be successful, or so our children and grand-children will turn out? Should we keep the main thing the main thing only to receive all the benefits and blessings that come from walking with God? Or should our motivation be different? What should motivate our walk with God person-ally, as a family, and corporately?

Our motivation for keeping the main thing the main thing must be *God alone*. He must be what we want more than anything else. If we are simply using our walk with God in order to be successful, righteous, and have things work out for us and our family, our walk with God is not rightfully motivated. Doing the right thing for the wrong reason is ultimately the sin of idolatry.

It is true that when we obey God's commandments and do things God's way, it will work. This is why many of us have experienced success in life from reading God's Word and doing what it says. But this does not necessarily mean that our obedience to God is rightfully motivated by true love for God and desiring Him above all else. It is all too possible simply to walk with God in order to receive His blessings – and this is wrong. It is sinful, " . . . and be sure your sin will find you out" (Numbers 32:23). God will not be mocked. If we sow the sin of idolatry, we will reap the whirlwind of pain, death, and destruction to all we hold dear because this is what sin does. It steals, kills, and destroys our relationships, our joy, our peace, and our hope. If unconfessed, it will destroy our very lives. Even if we try to dress sin up with "obedience," "religious show," and "apparent godliness," we cannot fool God. He knows what motivates us. He sees our hearts. "I, the LORD, search the heart, I try the reigns, even to give every man according to his ways . . ." (Jeremiah 17:10). We can keep no secrets from the Omniscient God. "For nothing is secret, that shall not be made manifest, neither anything hid, that shall not be made known and come abroad" (Luke 8:17).

Many people who have been wrongly motivated to pursue God have found that towards the end of their lives things start to unravel. Their kids and grandkids don't turn out, or rebel, or walk away from the faith altogether. Their businesses fall apart. Their marriages fall apart. Their life falls apart. The "Christian thing" doesn't work for them anymore. When that happens, anger, resentment, bitterness, discouragement, hopelessness, and sometimes apostasy results. This is because God is revealing their true motivation. They merely had the form of religion without the substance.

Children raised in Christian homes can spend so much of their lives participating in the form of religion that they can easily miss the main thing (which is God) and leave their homes wondering why we do all this "Christian stuff." They may get discouraged when they still encounter trouble in the world and feel like the "Christian thing" does not work for them. They may look at the world and think God is holding out on them and wonder why they are denying themselves all sorts of pleasures doing things the "Christian way." They may need to walk away for a season so God can show them that they were not pursing Him. They may have been simply complying or pursuing God's blessings or our approval. When God chooses to sanctify our children by revealing idols in their lives and then does the painful work of destroying them, we need to let God have his way with them. It is better for them to be sanctified directly by God than for them to think that doing Christian things saves them because it doesn't. Allowing them to figure out their true heart motivation is important for them and for us. True saving faith wants God more than His blessings.

The substance of true Christianity is God. The way to pursue God is to abide with Him personally, as a family, and corporately and want *Him* more than we want anything else. When we really live this way, we will be blessed beyond measure because we will possess what our soul desperately longs for which is intimacy with the Triune God. "Thou will show me the path of life: in thy presence is fullness of joy; at thy right hand there are pleasures for evermore!" (Psalm 16:11).

The main thing is not a method. It is not a program. It is not a checklist. It is not a way for us to rationalize our own traditions, convictions, and scruples. It is not something we can use to get things from God that we want. It's not the thing that we do just so we, or our families, will turn out. The main thing is wanting God more than His blessings. It is wanting God more than success. It is wanting God more than a happy marriage. It is wanting God more than we want our children and grandchildren to turn out. The main thing is God and abiding with Him because He must be our heart's desire and our first love!

Jesus said in Matthew 6:33, "But seek ye first the kingdom of God, and his righteousness; and all these things shall be added unto you." Note that He did not say that we should seek His kingdom first *so* all these things will be added unto us. We should not seek God first just so we will receive His blessings. Our motivation to seek God first must be God. Period. It must be to know Him. He must be our motivation. He must be our goal. He must be the ultimate thing we are seeking. When God is our motivation and our goal for walking with Him – in short, if God is our main thing – then all is well, all will be well, and all the things we need will be added to us for an abundant life.

Do you want things to work out? Do you want your children and grandchildren to be successful and thriving? Do you want your business to thrive? Do you want your marriage to thrive? Do you want abundant joy? Do you want the fear and doubt and insecurity that you have to go away? Do you want true peace? Do you want to sleep deeply and soundly at night? Do you want to approach the future with hope and optimism? THEN SEEK GOD, FOR GOD. "I have set before you life and death, blessing and cursing: therefore choose life, that both thou and thy seed may live: That thou mayest love the Lord thy God, and that thou mayest obey his voice: and that thou mayest cleave unto him, for he is thy life" (Deuteronomy 30:19-20).

Life and the ability to truly live are only found in a relationship with God. True love is only found when God is our first love. Abundant joy is found in God through obedience to His commands – and His command is ultimately that we love Him with everything we are. Peace that surpasses understanding is found in God as we keep our mind's attention and our heart's affection placed on Him. True rest is found in God alone. He has accomplished our salvation. God has promised to complete the good work He has started in us and in our children. We can trust Him with our life, our future, and with the lives of those we love when we seek Him alone, not the results. As we walk with God in a deep, close, intimate, covenantal relationship, we experience the abundant life He came to give us. In John 10:10, Jesus said, "I am come that they might have life, and that they might have it more abundantly." Jesus said, "Abide in me, and I in you...These things have I spoken unto you, that my joy might remain in you, and that your joy might be full" (John 15:4, 11).

CHAPTER 14

What do you believe? Are you really saved?

• • •

"Examine yourselves, whether ye be in the faith; prove your own selves. Know ye not your own selves, how that Jesus Christ is in you, except ye be reprobates?"

2 CORINTHIANS 13:5

ARE YOU SAVED? IS THE One True God of the Bible your God? How do you know? How can you be sure? Being religious and doing religious things will not save you. Going to church every Sunday cannot save you. Being a good Catholic, Baptist, Lutheran, Muslim, Mormon, Episcopalian, Buddhist, or Methodist does not save you. Being baptized does not save you. Just because your grandma, father, or mother went to heaven when they died does not mean you are going to heaven when you die. Reading your Bible does not mean you know God or are a true follower of Jesus Christ. Believing that there is a God does not mean He is your Savior. Praying to God does not mean that you have a personal saving relationship with Him. Living a moral and good life is not what is required by God to be saved. "Not every one that saith unto me, Lord, Lord, shall enter into the kingdom of heaven; but he that doeth the will of my Father which is in heaven" (Matthew 7:21).

Just because you say that you are a Christian does not mean that you are saved from hell. Many people think they are true Christians and say they are true Christians when they are not. Asking yourself if you are a Christian is the wrong question. People define the word Christian differently. Instead, ask yourself the most important question you have ever asked yourself while you are still alive and breathing. *Am I really saved?* This is a very important question. You need to know the answer, so read the book of Romans in your Bible. It is a matter of life and death.

The Bible tells us to examine ourselves. Do you believe in the Triune God of the Bible? "For there are three that bear record in heaven, the Father, the Word, and the Holy Ghost: and these three are one" (1 John 5:7). Do you believe the Father is God? "One God and Father of all, who is above all, and through all, and in you all" (Ephesians 4:6). Do you believe Jesus is God? "For in him dwelleth all the fulness of the Godhead bodily" (Colossians 2:9). Do you believe the Holy Spirit is God? "…why hath Satan filled thine heart to lie to the Holy Ghost . . . thou has not lied unto men, but unto God" (Acts 5:3-4). Do you believe that these three persons exist in One Godhead? "The grace of the Lord Jesus Christ, and the love of God, and the communion of the Holy Ghost, be with you all. Amen" (2 Corinthians 13:14).

Do you believe that God is the Creator? Genesis 1:1 says, "In the beginning God created the heaven and the earth."

Do you believe that Jesus came down from heaven and was conceived by the Holy Ghost in the womb of the virgin Mary? "Behold, a virgin shall conceive, and bear a son, and shall call his name Immanuel" (Isaiah 7:14). "And the angel said unto her, Fear not, Mary: for thou hast found favour with God. And, behold, thou shalt conceive in thy womb, and bring forth a son, and shalt call his name JESUS . . . Then said Mary unto the angel, How shall this be, seeing I know not a man? And the angel answered and said unto her, The Holy Ghost shall come upon thee, and the power of the Highest shall overshadow thee: therefore also that holy thing which shall be born of thee shall be called the Son of God" (Luke 1:30-31, 34-35). Do you believe that through this incredible event God became a man? Isaiah 9:6 says, "For unto us a child is born, unto us a son is given: and the government shall be upon his shoulder: and his name shall be called Wonderful Counsellor, The mighty God, The everlasting Father, The Prince of Peace."

Do you believe that Jesus lived a perfectly sinless life? "For he hath made him to be sin for us, who knew no sin . . ." (2 Corinthians 5:21). Do you believe that Jesus bled and died a cursed death on the cross? "And they crucified him... And set up over his head his accusation written, THIS IS

JESUS THE KING OF THE JEWS" (Matthew 27:35, 37). Do you believe that he was buried and after three days he rose from the dead? "In the end of the sabbath, as it began to dawn toward the first day of the week...behold, there was a great earthquake: for the angel of the Lord descended from heaven, and came and rolled back the stone from the door, and sat upon it... Fear not ye: for I know that ye seek Jesus, which was crucified. He is not here: for he is risen, as he said. Come see the place where the Lord lay. And go quickly, and tell his disciples that he is risen from the dead" (Matthew 28:1-2, 5-7).

Do you believe that you are sinful? Have you ever done anything wrong? Have you lied? Have you cheated? Have you judged? Have you worried? Have you complained? Have you taken the name of the Lord in vain? Have you looked lustfully at someone? Have you been greedy? Romans 3:23 says, "For all have sinned, and come short of the glory of God." Do you know that even if you are mostly a "good" or "moral" person, you are still a sinner in God's eyes? "For whosoever shall keep the whole law, and yet offend in one point, he is guilty of all" (James 2:10).

Do you believe in the Gospel? "I declare unto you the gospel . . . By which also ye are saved . . . how that Christ died for our sins according to the scriptures; And that he was buried, and that he rose again the third day according to the scriptures" (1 Corinthians 15:1-4). Do you believe the death, burial, and resurrection of Jesus Christ accomplished your salvation?

Do you think there is something you must add to what Jesus has done for you to be saved? What did Jesus mean when He was on the cross and He said, "It is finished" (John 19:30)? What does it mean when the Bible says in Ephesians 2:8-9, "For by grace are ye saved through faith; and that not of yourselves: it is the gift of God: Not of works, lest any man should boast?" It means Jesus paid it all. It is finished. Your salvation has been completely accomplished. Do you believe this?

If you believe it, have you confessed it with your mouth? Romans 10:9-10 says, "That if thou shalt confess with thy mouth the Lord Jesus, and shalt believe in thine heart that God hath raised him from the dead, thou shalt be saved. For with the heart man believeth unto righteousness; and with the mouth confession is made unto salvation."

Do you know God? What is He like? What are His attributes? Jeremiah 29:13 says that if you seek Him, you will find Him. Have you sought Him? Have you found Him? Do you know Him personally?

Do you love God? "And hope maketh not ashamed; because the love of God is shed abroad in our hearts by the Holy Ghost which is given unto us" (Romans 5:5). Have you set your affection on Him? Colossians 3:2 says, "Set your affection on things above, not on things on the earth." Is He your treasure? Do you desire Him? Do you spend time with Him? Do you talk to Him? Do you want to love Him with all your heart, soul, and strength? A man once asked Jesus what the greatest commandment in the law was, and

He answered, "Thou shalt love the Lord thy God with all thy heart, and with all thy soul, and with all thy mind. This is the first and great commandment. And the second is like unto it, Thou shalt love thy neighbor as thyself" (Matthew 22:36-39).

Do you love others? Jesus said in John 13:34-35, "A new commandment I give unto you, That ye love one another; as I have loved you, that ye also love one another. By this shall all men know that ye are my disciples, if ye have love one to another." 1 John 4 says, "Beloved, let us love one another: for love is of God; and every one that loveth is born of God, and knoweth God. He that loveth not knoweth not God; for God is love . . . And this commandment have we from him, That he who loveth God love his brother also" (1 John 4:7-8, 21).

Do you love God's Word? Psalm 119:97 says, "O how I love thy law! It is my meditation all the day." Do you read it? Do you study it? Do you apply it to your life? Do you hide God's Word in your heart so you will not sin against Him (Psalm 119:11)? Jesus said in John 8:31-32, "If ye continue in my word, then are ye my disciples indeed; And ye shall know the truth, and the truth shall make you free." Do you know the truth? Are you free?

Do you obey God's commandments? In John 14:15 Jesus said, "If ye love me, keep my commandments." Do you want to obey God? Are His commands burdensome to you? 1 John 5:3 says, "For this is the love of God, that we keep his commandments: and his commandments are not grievous."

Have you made a public profession of your faith by being baptized? Mark 16:16 says, "He that believeth and is baptized shall be saved; but he that believeth not shall be damned." Jesus said in Matthew 28:19-20, "Go ye therefore, and teach all nations, baptizing them in the name of the Father, and of the Son, and of the Holy Ghost: Teaching them to observe all things whatsoever I have commanded you. . . ."

Do you see fruit in your life? Galatians 5:22-24 says, "But the fruit of the Spirit is love, joy, peace, longsuffering, gentleness, goodness, faith, meekness, temperance: against such there is no law. And they that are Christ's have crucified the flesh with the affections and lusts." Do you lust after the things of the world? Jesus said in Matthew 7:20, "Wherefore by their fruits ye shall know them."

Do you see a change in your heart? Ezekiel 36:26-27 says, "A new heart also will I give you, and a new spirit will I put within you: and I will take away the stony heart out of your flesh, and I will give you an heart of flesh. And I will put my spirit within you, and cause you to walk in my statues, and ye shall keep my judgments, and do them." If not, is your heart hard, stubborn, or rebellious?

Are you just conforming outwardly by living a moral life, going to church, praying a prayer, and being baptized but not truly believing in God for your salvation? Galatians 6:7 says, "Do not be deceived; God is not mocked: for whatsoever a man soweth, that shall he also reap." 1 Samuel 16:7 says, "...for the Lord seeth not as man seeth; for man looketh on the outward appearance, but the Lord looketh on the heart." Ecclesiastes 12:14 says, "For God shall bring every work into judgment, with every secret thing, whether it be good, or whether it be evil." Jesus said in Matthew 7:21-23, "Not every one that saith unto me, Lord, Lord, shall enter into the kingdom of heaven; but he that doeth the will of my Father which is in heaven. Many will say to me in that day, Lord, Lord, have we not prophesied in thy name? and in thy name have cast out devils? and in thy name done many wonderful works? And then will I profess unto them, I never knew you: depart from me, ye that work iniquity." Do you know God? Do you believe? Do you love Him? Are you going through the motions or have you yielded your life and heart to Him?

Are you really saved? Are you in the fold of the Good Shepherd? Can you hear His voice? Do you follow Him? Jesus said, "I am the good shepherd...and I lay down my life for the sheep . . . No man taketh it from me, but I lay it down of myself. I have power to lay it down, and I have power to take it again . . . My sheep hear my voice, and I know them, and they follow me: And I give unto them eternal life; and they shall never perish, neither shall any man pluck them out of my hand" (John 10:14-15, 18, 27-28). God saves you! If you really believe and have professed sincerely with your mouth your true faith in the Triune God of the Bible through belief in the finished work of Jesus on the cross, then no one can pluck you out of the saving hand of God. You are saved! The Holy Spirit is within you. "... no man speaking by the Spirit of God calleth Jesus accursed: and that no man can say that Jesus is the Lord, but by the Holy Ghost" (1 Corinthians 12:3). The Holy Spirit within you bears testimony that you are a child of God. "For as many as are led by the Spirit of God, they are the sons of God. For ye have not received the spirit of bondage again to fear; but ye have received the Spirit of adoption, whereby we cry, Abba, Father. The Spirit itself beareth witness with our spirit, that we are the children of God" (Romans 8:14-16).

Do you believe in God but live rebelliously before Him by refusing to live according to His revealed will for you? If you answered yes, know that you are living in sin. It is not well with you. Your sin will find you out (Numbers 32:23). You are sowing the wind, but you will reap the whirlwind (Hosea 8:7). You are in a very scary and extremely dangerous place. "Sin is the transgression of the law" (1 John 3:4). Know also that your sins have separated you from your God (Isaiah 59:2). To one extent or another, all of us have been, are, or will be in this position even if we are believers. "If we say that we have no sin, we deceive ourselves, and the truth is not in us" (1 John 1:8). If you cannot perceive sin in your life, you may need to ask God to show you. "Search me, O God, and know my heart: try me, and know my thoughts: And see if there be any wicked way in me, and lead me in the way everlasting" (Psalm 139:23-24). When we perceive that we are living rebelliously before God, the only response is to confess that sin to God. When we do, we receive the cleansing power of His forgiveness. "If we confess our sins, he is faithful and just to forgive us our sins, and to cleanse us from all unrighteousness" (1 John 1:9). With our fellowship with God restored, we need to abide with Him, love Him, and consequently obey Him. John 14:15 says, "If you love me, keep my commandments." Jesus indicates in Luke 11:24-26 that it is simply not enough to take sin out of our lives because it will return with a vengeance. We need to replace our sin and rebellion with faithful obedience to God that flows from our love for Him. This is our duty, but it should not feel like a duty. Rather, it should be the natural outworking of our love for God. It should be our greatest joy.

If the Holy Spirit has convicted you and shown you that you are not saved, call upon God for salvation right now! "Look unto me, and be ye saved, all the ends of the earth: for I am God, and there is none else" (Isaiah 45:22). It does not matter what words you use. Call upon Him for salvation now and do not delay! You may not get another chance! "Behold, now is the day of salvation" (2 Corinthians 6:2). "To day if ye will hear his voice, harden not your hearts" (Hebrews 4:7). Know that if you have called upon God, you are saved, and you are safe! "For whosoever shall call upon the name of the Lord shall be saved" (Romans 10:13).

CHAPTER 15

Keep the Main Thing the Main Thing

• • •

"Abide in me, and I in you. As the branch cannot bear fruit of itself, except it abide in the vine; no more can ye, except ye abide in me."

JOHN 15:4

IF YOU ARE SAVED, THEN you should spend the rest of your life keeping the main thing the main thing. The main thing is God – God alone. Get to know Him, enjoy Him, and walk with Him. Make God your heart's desire.

When God is your first priority, you will keep Him at the center of your life, and He will be the goal you are striving for in all you do. Then, you will have joy, purpose, and meaning in your life. Jesus said, "Abide in me . . . keep my commandments . . . These things have I spoken unto you, that my joy might remain in you, and that your joy might be full" (John 15:4, 10, 11). The analogy Jesus uses in John 15 is that of grapes connected to a vine. Grapes cannot grow and thrive in and of themselves. They need to be connected to the vine. Similarly, we cannot grow and thrive spiritually unless we are connected to Jesus, the Vine and the Source of all of our spiritual nourishment. A life lived to its fullest is a life lived hidden with Christ in God (Colossians 3:3). He is the Source of life. Acts 17:28 says, "For in him we live, and move, and have our being." These Scripture passages teach us that we cannot live life to the fullest extent possible unless we are abiding with God.

If abiding with God is your main thing, all is well. You can be a farmer, a doctor, a policeman, a teacher, a lawyer, or anything God calls you to and have a meaningful and joyful life if God is your main thing. You can be married or single, and you will live an abundant and full life if God is your main thing. You can breastfeed or bottle feed, send your children to school or educate them at home, and choose to go to college or not. Above all, you can relax. You will not have to look to the right or left because God is your main thing, and that means all will be well. You are free to live the life God has called you to, and you are free to let others live the lives God has called them to. He will lead and guide you, and He will lead and guide everyone else who is abiding in and walking with Him. There is no need to judge. God wants Christians everywhere. He loves variety. He may want you to have one child, or twelve, or twenty, or none at all. He may want you to live in China. He may want you to live in the Bronx, or He may want you to live in a quiet, normal neighborhood.

Keeping the main thing the main thing involves walking with God personally, as a family, and corporately. It means abiding with God personally in a deep, close, and intimate covenantal relationship. It means abiding with God as a family by reading the Bible together, praying together, and worshipping together. It means abiding with God in church on Sunday by worshipping God with other believers. And it means abiding with God all the time, as you live your life, knowing that the Holy Spirit indwells you.

As you abide with God, the Holy Spirit within you will teach you and bring God's Word to your mind, for this is His job (John 14:26). He will then help you apply the Word of God to your life. "...work out your own salvation with fear and trembling. For it is God which worketh in you both to will and to do of his good pleasure" (Philippians 2:12-13). "And I will put my spirit within you, and cause you to walk in my statutes, and ye shall keep my judgments, and do them" (Ezekiel 36:27). Right behavior will flow from your rightly oriented heart.

Christianity is not about following a list of rules or a formula. It is about knowing God and doing everything God has called you to do each day with Him and for His glory. God has called us to many different things. Jesus said keeping the main thing is seeking Him first. In Matthew 6:33, Jesus said, "But seek ye first the kingdom of God, and his righteousness; and all these things shall be added unto you."

Keeping God as the main thing in your life will be the hardest thing you will ever do. It is simple, but it is not easy.

Seek Him first. Keep God central. Make God the goal of all you do. Strive to know and enjoy God more everyday. Do everything with God and for His glory. Know that keeping the main thing the main thing is what Jesus wants for you. "Abide in me, and I in you" (John 15:4). Also know that the Holy Spirit is within you, and He will help you. "...he dwelleth with you, and shall be in you" (John 14:17).

When you keep the main thing the main thing, you will find that you are living in heaven right here on earth. Revelation 21:3 says, "Behold, the tabernacle of God is with men, and he will dwell with them, and they shall be his people, and God himself shall be with them, and be their God." When God is your main thing, all is well and all will be well!

God is everything! He is our conquering King. He is our Lord. He is our Bridegroom. He is our best friend. He is our strength. He is our song. He is our co-laborer. He is our peace. He is our joy. He is our hope. He is our comforter. He is our refuge. He is our wisdom. He is our good Father. He is our loving Father. He is our heavenly Father. God wants all of you, and He wants to be all to you. He wants to be your all in all. Make God everything, and you will have everything.

Where is this all going, and why is it important? Our God is doing a great work on the earth. As a result of His Son Jesus' death, burial, and resurrection, all things are made new (2 Corinthians 5:17). The cleansing power of God given to us and to the world through the power and work of the Holy Spirit is flowing out from His throne and is flooding this whole world; one day it will flood the entire world (Ezekiel 47:1-5). The tree of life, Jesus Christ, is growing on that river and bearing much fruit and leaves that will heal the nations (Revelation 22:2). While the greatest fulfillment of these passages is still to come, progress toward that goal is ongoing now through the work of Jesus Christ within His people and this world. "For he must reign, till he hath put all enemies under his feet . . . For he hath put all things under his feet" (1 Corinthians 15:25, 27).

Psalm 1 tells us that the blessed refuse to walk in the counsel of the ungodly, stand in the way of sinners, or sit in the seat of the scornful and are instead delighting and meditating in the law of the Lord day and night. Those people will be like trees planted by rivers of water bringing forth fruit and leaves that will not wither. Whatever that person does will prosper. Does this language sound familiar? This is the same imagery that is used in Ezekiel and in Revelation.

When we consider all of these passages together, we see that we have been ordained by God to heal and restore this world. We are the fruits coming from the Source of Life, Jesus Christ. We are the leaves that will heal the nations because we are in Christ, the Tree of Life. God is accomplishing and will continue to accomplish His plans for the world through us. All power and authority has been given to Jesus Christ. Therefore, we have been called to go into the world and make disciples of all nations. We have been called to baptize them in the name of the Father, the Son, and the Holy Spirit, teach them to observe everything God has commanded us to do, and recognize that Jesus is with us always until the end of the world (Matthew 28:18-20). This is why we have been placed in families, in churches, in neighborhoods, in nations, and in this world.

But how can we heal the nations if we are withered? How can we bear fruit when we have no sustenance? How can we baptize the nations and bring them into the church of God when we are not worshipping Him corporately in spirit and in truth? How can we disciple our families and the nations and teach them to observe what God has commanded when we do not know and meditate on the Word of God ourselves? *Ultimately, how can we give what we do not have ourselves?*

"Abide in me, and I in you," Jesus says to us. "As the branch cannot bear fruit of itself, except it abide in the vine; no more can ye, except ye abide in me. I am the vine, ye are the branches: He that abideth in me, and I in him, the same bringeth forth much fruit: for without me ye can do nothing . . . Herein is my Father glorified, that ye bear much fruit; so shall ye be my disciples" (John 15:4-5, 8).

This is why we *absolutely must* abide with God *individually* and why *you and I* must recognize that we can only bear fruit if we walk with God by reading, meditating on, and applying His Word and talk to Him continually in prayer. In short, this is why we keep the main thing the main thing. The main thing is God and our relationship with Him. We abide with Him personally, within our families, and corporately in the body of Christ. As we abide, God will give us everything He has promised to us as heirs and recipients of His covenant, and His Spirit will help and enable us to respond with faithful and dutiful obedience and love for Him and for others.

When we abide with God in His Word and in His presence, we are filled. Our every need is satisfied – physically and spiritually. Then, we respond in obedience that is not out of a sense of duty or performance but because *we love our Savior and can't help but want to please Him.* And it is only then that we can truly live. "In this was manifested the love of God toward us, because that God sent his only begotten Son into the world, that we might live through him" (1 John 4:9). This is anything but a call to individualism because when you are truly walking with God, your natural response is to love those around you because you are filled to overflowing with the love of God (1 John 4:7).

It is when you abide with God that you can truly thrive and bear fruit. You will not be withered or thirsty, but you will have the water of life flowing from your soul, penetrating your entire being, and springing up into everlasting life (John 4:14). When you are abiding in the life-sustaining, life-giving, cleansing power of God, you are abiding by the river that is flowing from His throne and will thrive and bear fruit. God will sustain, carry, and support you all the days of your life from your youth to your old age (Isaiah 46:4).

You will now be able to go in the full resurrection power of God and sustain your children, your family, your neighbors, your brothers and sisters in Christ, your colleagues, and this broken world with the fruit and leaves of healing from the Lord Jesus Christ, the Tree of Life. You will die someday, but you will die rejoicing because you are departing to be with Christ (Philippians 1:23). God will continue to save individuals, families, and nations. And one day, as Isaiah 11:9 tells us, the earth will be full of the knowledge of the Lord, as the waters cover the sea. The Lord Jesus will return and destroy our last enemy – death (1 Corinthians 15:26). And we will enter into eternity with our God and abide with Him forever and ever.

Father God, we come to you and surrender our lives. They are not ours. They are Yours. We have been crucified with Christ, and yet we live. Yet it is not us, Jesus, but it is You within us. The life we live now, we live by faith in You who loved us and died for us. O Lord, help us to abide with You! Help us to keep the main thing the main thing! In the name of Jesus we pray, because there is no other name given among men whereby we must be saved. And now, we pray the words that Your Son taught us to pray:

"Our Father which art in heaven,
Hallowed be thy name.
Thy kingdom come,
Thy will be done in earth, as it is in heaven.
Give us this day our daily bread.

And forgive us our debts, as we forgive our debtors.
And lead us not into temptation, but deliver us from evil:
For thine is the kingdom, and the power,
and the glory, for ever.
Amen."

Matthew 6:9-13

76030632R00051

Made in the USA
Lexington, KY
19 December 2017